PROPERTY: THE 100 BEST WAYS
TO BUY AND SELL

Every effort has been made to contact the copyright holders of material reproduced in this book. In cases where these efforts have been unsuccessful, the copyright holders are asked to contact the publishers directly.

PUBLISHED IN 2009 BY BOOK REPUBLIC.
Office 19, Dunboyne Business Park, Dunboyne, Co. Meath, Ireland.
http://www.bookrepublic.ie

CONTACT INFO AND SALES
http://www.100bestways.com

ISBN: 978-1-907221-00-2

Copyright for text and pictures © 2009 Ken Madden & Ken Buggy.

A CIP catalogue record for this book is available from the British Library.

PROPERTY:
THE 100 BEST WAYS TO BUY AND SELL

Ken Madden & Ken Buggy

 Book Republic

MADBUG PRESS

ACKNOWLEDGEMENTS

With thanks to Pauline, Cathleen, Neil, Dermot, Jean, Tommy, Douglas, Simon and everybody else who helped.

INTRODUCTION

None of us can pass an estate agents window without stopping to look. Like the home-making instincts of animals who all want security and comfort, we all want the ideal. Unlike animals, however, we want something more.

What is it?

Within this simple book you'll find answers, delivered in a sensible and inexpensive way. Easy to understand and quick to act upon, it will undoubtedly make you more informed about the property market. It will certainly make you smile.

Buy it now, take it home, and read it as quick as you dare.

"This is the first half, boss."

Will the furniture from your previous house fit, and will the removals truck get to the front door?

"We will be taking one or two pieces with us."

In most cases, if the furniture is any good, the sellers will take it with them! Unless you're badly stuck, ask for VACANT possession.

However, always keep an eye out for a priceless antique!

"If I lean the tower to the left, you can see the sea!"

An architect will examine your site and draw up plans for your new home. Some architects also do extensions.

"Looks lovely from the front, dear."

Examine the entire property, particularly the sides and rear, which may not have been cared for as much.

"Slight dampness in the walls but nothing to worry about."

Ask if the house has a damp course. If not, modern methods can fix this relatively inexpensively.

"It has a different postal code, so of course it's more expensive."

Location can be VERY important when you are buying. So find out why!

With the vendor's permission, use a video recorder or camera. It will help to remind you of the property when you get home.

If you have pets, make sure the house and it's location are suitable. It's a home for them also!

"Caveat Emptor."

The seller is not responsible in any way for the quality of the property being sold or any defects found thereafter. So: BUYER BEWARE!

"We're looking for something in concrete."

Both timber framed and concrete built homes are popular. Be aware of what type you are buying—and the advantages that each has to offer.

Be sure to understand all the jargon used and if not, don't be afraid to ask.

"Now dear, you tell those silly men about the right of way and where to put their pike."

Lots of rural properties have rights-of-way, which may provide access to the house or adjacent lands. Make yourself aware of such situations and who is responsible for their upkeep.

"Are we too early?"

It's worthwhile arriving ahead of time for your viewing appointment. You'll have an opportunity to view the locale, study the neighbourhood and enjoy more time on the property before the agent rushes to the next appointment. And if you're running late, always let the agent know!

"And of course they have provided swift access to city routes."

Firstly consider if the location is suitable to you and your needs, and then make an appointment to view!

Check floorboards—are they solid, dry and well maintained? Most fungi really do thrive on rising damp.

"Geo Thermals? My Fred wears his all the time."

Is the house energy efficient?

Consider engaging the services of a mortgage broker. A mortgage broker is associated with several lenders and may find you a better deal.

Most agents have web sites or use property search engines. Have a look over these sites to see what's available.

"*Trés petit, trés chic, Madam.*"

Show houses sometimes use smaller furniture, such as two seater settees. This can be deceptive when you are estimating the size of the room. Bring a measuring tape with you!

*"So you think the house made
with straw will blow down?"*

If you intend to build, always go for a pre-
planning meeting with the local authority. There,
you will find out what type of house you will get
permission to build, and perhaps other helpful
information.

When meeting with the council planning officials, ask what they mean by "traditional" and draw your plans accordingly.

"They told us it was a skip."

When viewing—wear clothing and footwear appropriate to the condition of the house or site.

"Are you two connected to the mains?"

Find out what services the property has—and if there is a maintenance or local authority charge for the use and upkeep.

"With the advantage of nearby parking."

KENBUGGY

Most rural properties have private on-site parking; but townhouses may not. Don't discount a property if it hasn't got parking.

Buying or leasing a parking space in a convenient car park may be a suitable option.

"Bungalow Bliss / Blitz!"

Built up areas may not be attractive to everyone but they sometimes suit couples with younger families.

"As an electrician I must warn you:
that I'll be here at 9.00am on Monday."

If you are worried about the electrics, call your
local electrician. He'll be happy to help you.

"Can we talk carbon foot print?"

Does the house fulfil your energy requirements?

Other potential buyers may jump in with an offer, even though you may have already agreed a sale.

So don't hang about—finish off the deal promptly.

"*This is your last chance to leave a deposit.*"

When you agree to purchase—don't hang about. Place a deposit with the agent and move the deal forward.

An experienced and up-to-date surveyor is an important part of the buying process.

Consider what they tell you, then be brave and make your own decision.

"The seals around the bath are all intact."

Check for a quality finish around baths and showers. Leaks may have caused damage over a period of time.

Some sellers paint their home in advance of a sale, but look out for paintwork that may be covering up damp patches.

Try to be specific in your request with the estate agent.

"Just watch the PSI — don't let her blow!"

Check the age of the boilers. Have they been serviced and well maintained?

" Arise! You now have Planning Permission."

Planning permission can be a difficult area for the novice. It's wise to hire a professional to carry out this work for you.

"Our family is expanding - even as we speak..."

Always think of the future and plan the purchase of your house accordingly.

You may need extra bedrooms, a home office or a large garden!

"Looks like a bankers draught."

If you are thinking of buying, make an appointment to meet with your bank manager and establish how much money they are likely to lend you.

Be open minded when trying to buy a property.
It's almost impossible to find the perfect home!

"It's in an arty location."

Clever buyers choose an area that's up and coming.

If possible, it is important to visit the property location on different days and times.

What might seem beautiful one day, may not appear so appealing on another.

"3 for the price of 2."

If a property is being sold unusually cheap, there's usually a reason! A little investigating will get you answers and it can be good news as much as bad.

"Little Black and Decker will work wonders."

If the location is right, it's okay to buy a wreck. As long as you have the means and enthusiasm to renovate and refurbish.

"The door is jammed and I can't open the window."

Check that the windows and doors open and close correctly—and look out for signs of deterioration.

"Our solar panels will give you a bath or a pot of tea."

Ask about solar panels, pellet boilers, stoves and other eco features.

In emerging foreign markets, buyers may find a bargain property.

But beware—make sure to hire a good solicitor if buying abroad.

"Anything catching your eye yet dear?"

Many buyers like to peruse online the various properties on the market—so make sure your agent has placed yours on the internet.

Check the electrics. The sockets, light switches and fuse board will tell you if the property has had a decent upgrading. And if you're planning on a refit, don't be afraid to include new electrics in your costing. Keep it safe!

"We're wondering about downsizing."

Moving to a smaller house can save on maintenance and heating costs and can earn you some money from the sale.

"Me and Frank are looking for something in the Buyers Market Section."

Don't be afraid to tell the agent that you have a budget.

"Just ask the neighbours to duck when you are doing the washing."

If the garden is small, learn from your neighbours! It may be worth looking at their layout from an upstairs window.

KENBUGGY

When you are granted planning permission, you may have to make a contribution to the local authority. It's best to check in advance how the authority calculates this amount.

"See ... great pressure!"

Check that taps run well, that toilets flush properly
and that the electrics work.

"This property is on a gentle slope."

Check what direction the house is facing. If it is on a sloping site, pay particular attention to the foundations.

When selling, be realistic about the value of your property and take advice from your estate agent as to what may be achieved in the market.

It's time to view—put your best foot forward.
Clear away any personal effects; take the washing
in off the clothesline. Present your house in a
clean and attractive way.

"We go in at dawn."

Buyers will send out a surveyor to check and evaluate the property and its condition.

Solicitors no longer wear funny clothes.

When buying or selling, you will need the services of a solicitor. You need the most comprehensive service for what is your biggest deal so use the best you can afford.

"And here we have a log."

Most homeowners now keep a log of essential and other works carried out on their property. It's a very useful document to present to potential buyers.

"And what did you do?"

Pay those handling your sale or purchase properly. They will do a better job and give you more of their time.

When selling, ask your solicitor to prepare the deeds and other such documents in advance.

If you're extending, get planning permission, and then build according to your permit.

Be honest and open about every aspect of your property and it's sale. When it comes to closing a sale there should be no last minute difficulties.

Your agent should market your property, not necessarily to the widest audience, but to the "correct" audience.

KENBUGGY

"I'd like this in a prime position."

Ask your agent for a prime position on the window with a nice picture of your home.

"Smells nice."

The smell of baked bread or fresh coffee can give
your house a "homely ambiance" for a viewing.

Keep an eye on your brochure in the estate agents window—ensure its not obscured or faded by the sun.

KENBUGGY

Consider having a professional photographer to photograph your property. It will make the brochure of your property stand out from the rest.

"I'm just doing a little conveyancing officer."

The work undertaken by your solicitor in relation to your sale is known as conveyancing.

It's important to use a good solicitor who will make sure that all parts of the contract are present and correct.

"So, how can we help you?"

It's most useful to have details to hand of all the facilities available locally.

Tidy up your garden—mow the lawn, plant some flowers or put out some hanging baskets and pots.

"OK people! Let's talk database."

Ask your agent to send an e-mail with details of your property to his online clients.

There are many ways in which to market your property. Talk to your estate agent and be open to his or her ideas.

Open houses are becoming more popular in city locations. Being similar to a show house, the property is advertised as being open for viewing for a few hours, usually at weekends.

" ... and of course it's well ventilated."

Ventilate your house—get rid of cooking smells long before the clients arrive.

"OK sir, can you run the Christian/ Lion thing past me again?"

Many newspapers and magazines run features and editorials, and the journalists always like properties with an interesting history.

" And of course over here ..."

Be honest—don't try to hide problems or faults.

"We never felt the need to
fit a burglar alarm."

Security systems are important for peace of mind,
and most insurers give a discount if you have
one.

"That's just Spot's idea of a welcome."

Not all potential buyers like noisy dogs so get someone to look after them for the day.

"We're not in a rush to sell."

If it's for sale, it's for sale! Always be ready if the right buyer comes along.

"It's the people to see the house."

Turn off the radio and television before the clients come to view.

Before you sell it's time to finish off some of those irritating jobs.

Check that all the bulbs fit well and are working.

" ... and this is the loo."

KENBUGGY

Always have your house spotlessly clean for a viewing. There should be no part of the house that your estate agent would be embarrassed to show to the clients.

If you keep pets, your property may need an extra effort when it comes to cleaning.

If your property looks beautiful and is perfectly presented, it will be easier for the estate agent to excite potential buyers.

Let the agent do the selling. They are best skilled at showing off your property.

"Dare yare now luv."

If you have permission to build a detached garage, and haven't yet built it—do so before selling. It usually enhances the value of a property.

"Somehow I think she'll take more than the litre Jim."

First impressions are vital. A coat of paint, both inside, and outside, can make a huge difference to a house.

"Hey guys!"

KENBUGGY

If you have converted a small bedroom into an office or alternative space, reconvert it prior to selling.

Many buyers base their requirements and value on the number of bedrooms.

"Let's not mention slow burner here."

Be patient—some houses take longer to sell than others.

"That's nice dear."

Strategically placed fresh flowers or plants can brighten up a house—just be sure to remove any dead ones!

"I think we may have overdone the warm welcome/light the fire thing"

It's important to create a nice atmosphere in your home when a potential buyer is calling—so if it's cold outside, have a nice fire lighting.

"It's got a downstairs loo, Mavis."

There's a buyer for every property and some may see an aspect that you previously have not—so highlight all elements of your property to their fullest.

"This sealed bid thing was all your idea."

If a property is being sold by tender, offers are placed in an envelope and sent to the agent.

"We'll only sell if they are very nice."

Yes—it's your home, and you've hopefully given it a lot of love and care.

But once you decide to sell, turn your thoughts away from who its new owner may be and focus on your new abode.

"I don't need to do anything."

It's "your" house to sell. So have it in show house condition for viewings.

Some fresh paint, or perhaps a new carpet, along with good presentation will add substantially to the value of your house.

Whether buying or selling, always make yourself
aware of the costs and taxes involved.

Read everything thoroughly.

Gather as much information as you can—and read through the details thoroughly.

"*Gone to the gentleman in the cheap suit.*"

If you intend to bid for a property at an auction, you must make sure to carry out all checks and reports; have your solicitor review the deeds and contract; and have your deposit ready.

This way, if you are the highest bidder, you'll be able to sign the contracts on the day!

If you want to talk to, or meet with your solicitor, then make an appointment and do so. Don't get fobbed off by the secretary!